I0616128

Nerdy, Dirty, and Tasteless STAR WARS JOKES IV

Nerdy, Dirty, and Tasteless STAR WARS JOKES IV

John Szeluga

Christopher J. Sorrentino

No generative artificial intelligence (AI) was used in the writing of this work. The author expressly prohibits any entity from using this publication for purposes of training AI technologies to generate text, including without limitation technologies that are capable of generating works in the same style or genre as this publication. The author reserves all rights to license uses of this work for generative AI training and development of machine learning language models.

To all the creative minds behind Star Wars, and countless joke tellers throughout time and space, without whom this book could never exist.

Contents

Acknowledgments

Christine, thank you for thoroughly proof-reading multiple drafts of this book despite not getting most of the jokes.

Joe Imburgio and Manny Rondon, thank you both for honestly telling us what did and didn't (and maybe still doesn't) work.

Mike Finoia, thanks for always being there to talk things through.

Shoutout to Wookieepedia and all the fans who contribute.

To our familes, thank you for your constant love and support. Kids, **DO NOT** read this book until you turn 18!

Bantha Fodder

What's the difference between a Jawa and a bucket of shit?

The bucket.

*   *   *

You gotta hand it to Jawas.

They can't reach it on their own.

*   *   *

Three Jawas walk into a bar.

A Wookiee steps over it.

*   *   *

A Jawa stumbles out of the cantina.

He was a little drunk.

What's the difference between a thieving Jawa and a yeast infection?

One is a cunning runt.

How is having an interrogation droid in your detention cell like sharing a bed with a Jawa?

You might feel a little prick.

What do you call a group of Jawas?

Target practice.

What do you get when you cross a Tusken Raider with a Jawa?

Nothing. There are some things even Sand People won't do.

*   *   *

Did you hear about the Tusken Raider beauty pageant winner?

Me neither.

What do you call a hundred Tusken Raiders cast out into space?

A good start.

How do you get a Tusken Raider pregnant?

Dress her up like Anakin's mom.

What does a Tusken Raider do for fun?

Beats the hell out of Shmi.

* * *

Young Luke is walking across the desert with his uncle Owen when he spots a bantha. Luke points and says, "Uncle Owen, what's that hanging from the bantha?"

Uncle Owen looks and says, "That's the bantha's long, brown fur."

"No, not that," says Luke. "What's that hanging near the back?"

"That's the bantha's tail," answers Uncle Owen.

Frustrated, Luke points again and says, "No, what's THAT?"

Uncle Owen realizes what Luke is pointing at and answers, "Well, Luke, that's the bantha's penis."

"But, Uncle Owen," says Luke, "I asked Aunt Beru the same thing when we saw a bantha yesterday and she told me it was nothing."

"Luke," says Uncle Owen, "you have to understand that your Aunt Beru is a very spoiled woman."

*   *   *

Furballs and Walking Carpets

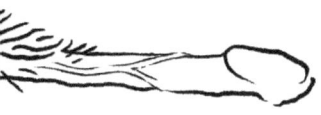

How did Wicket cross the road?

Ewoked to the other side.

Why do Ewoks giggle when they run?

The grass tickles their balls.

Did you hear about the Wookiee who dated an Ewok?

He was nuts over her.

*   *   *

Why did the Ewok fall out of the tree?

Because it was dead.

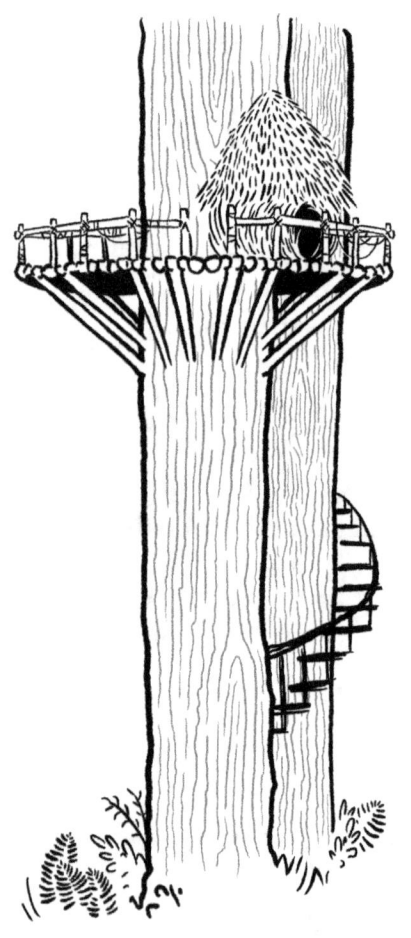

What do you get when you cross an Ewok with a Toong?

George Lucas.

15

What do you call a Wookiee with four eyes?

A Wookiiiiee.

How do you kill a hundred fleas in one go?

Slap a Wookiee in the face.

How do you kill a thousand fleas in one go?

Punch a Wookiee in the balls.

How do you kill a million fleas in one go?

Set a Wookiee on fire.

What do you do with a Wookiee in your bed?

Whatever he wants.

*   *   *

What pops out when a Wookiee fucks a porg?

The porg's eyes.

What do Wookiees use as cock rings?

Flea collars.

* * *

What has four arms, four legs, two heads, is covered in fur, and smells like hot shit?

Two Wookiees butt-fucking.

* * *

A Wookiee walks into a bar with a porg on his shoulder.

"What can I get for you?" asks the bartender.

The porg says, "Two glasses of Jawa Juice, please."

Amazed, the bartender replies, "Wow! That thing's amazing! Where'd ya get it?"

"Kashyyyk," says the porg. "They've got millions of 'em."

*   *   *

After the Battle of Endor, Han and Lando vow to stay in touch.

"What are you doing for Life Day?" asks Han.

"No plans," replies Lando.

"Leia and I are going to Chewie's place. You should join us. I'm sure Chewie won't mind."

"I don't know..." says Lando. "Will it be just the three of you?"

"No," says Han. "There's also Chewie's wife, Malla. She's the best. His son is Lumpy. Sweet kid. And Chewie's dad is a bit of a crank, but I think you'd get a kick out of him. He's Itchy."

"Forget it," says Lando.

"C'mon," says Han. "Chewie's wife is making Bantha Surprise!"

"As tasty as that sounds," says Lando, "if Chewie's dad is itchy and his son is lumpy, I'm not going over there until those two see a vet!"

Why do they call Chewbacca's father Itchy?

Because no one ever cleans the cum off his weird VR porn chair.

Why is Chewbacca's son Lumpy?

Because he doesn't listen.

Nerf Herders and Moof Milkers

What's the difference between Binaca and Panaka?

Binaca is the spray that freshens your breath, and Panaka is that asshole who stinks up a movie.

*   *   *

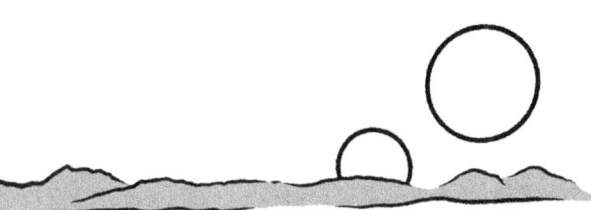

A lonely moisture farmer named Cliegg Lars wins Shmi Skywalker's freedom in a bet with her enslaver, Watto. Cliegg puts Shmi on the back of his eopie and heads for home.

While traveling through the desert, the eopie stops walking, looks back at Cliegg and Shmi, and lets out a loud, stinky fart. Cliegg, clearly irritated, shouts "That's one!" and the eopie starts walking again.

After a little while more, the eopie stops and farts a second time. Cliegg, starting to get angry, shouts "That's two!" and the eopie starts walking again.

Getting closer to the moisture farm, the eopie stops and farts a third time.

Cliegg, now furious, grabs his blaster and dismounts. He steps in front of the eopie, shouts "That's three!" and shoots the eopie dead. Shmi, horrified, screams at Cliegg.

"That poor innocent creature! How can you be so cruel?! You're a monster!"

Cliegg turns toward Shmi, raises a finger and says, "That's one."

Why couldn't Cliegg Lars save Shmi Sky-walker from the Tusken Raiders?

He didn't have a leg to stand on.

Why did the Lars family moisture farm shut down?

They were operating with a skeleton crew.

Why does Luke keep having nightmares about Uncle Owen and Aunt Beru?

Because skeletons are scary.

Why does Dexter Jettster have four arms?

There's one to scratch his ass, one to scratch his balls, and two to make you a sandwich.

* * *

What's big, gray, hairy, and smelly and hangs out behind the cantina bar?

Ackmena's nut sack.

* * *

A Coruscanti man walks into the Galactic Courts of Justice Building and tells the clerk he wants to change his name. The clerk isn't that eager to help until she asks the man his name and the man replies, "My name is Stinky Palpatine."

Upon hearing such an awful name, the clerk is sympathetic and decides to help the poor guy. "What do you want to change your name to?" asks the clerk.

"Stinky Shitz," replies the man.

Pathetic
Life Forms

Did you ever hear the song John Williams composed for a deleted eopie fight scene in *The Phantom Menace*?

It's called "Duel of the Farts."

What makes this joke book worse than *The Phantom Menace*?

There's only one eopie fart joke in *The Phantom Menace*.

What do you get when you cross a Gungan with a Kowakian monkey-lizard?

A stupid Kowakian monkey-lizard.

* * *

A Rodian and a Gungan jump off a cliff to see who'll hit the bottom first. Who wins?

The galaxy.

A young Gungan rushes home to tell his father about something he learned from the new teacher droid at school.

"Dada!" shouts the excited Gungan. "Did yousa know dat Tatooine and Mon Cala have twin suns?"

"Nosa!" replies the Gungan's father. "Mesa didn't even know deysa married!"

*   *   *

What did the Gungan get on his algebra test?

Drool.

*   *   *

Why don't they make ice in Otoh Gunga anymore?

The Gungan with the recipe died.

* * *

How do you get a one-armed Gungan out of a tree?

Wave at him.

* * *

Why do little Gungan girls throw chunks of gooberfish down their pants?

So they can smell like big Gungan girls.

* * *

Did you hear about the Gungan rebel they sent to blow up a TIE Fighter?

He burnt his lips on the exhaust port.

* * *

What are the hardest three years of a Gungan's life?

First grade.

* * *

In a diplomatic meeting between the Gungans and the Naboo, Boss Nass laid out his plans for the Gungans to explore the galaxy, starting with a mission to Naboo's sun, the star Naboo.

"You can't travel to the sun!" exclaimed Sio Bibble, governor of Naboo. "You'll burn alive!"

"No, no, nosa!" replied Boss Nass. "Wesa okeyday. Wesa bees goen at night!"

* * *

Newly appointed Junior Representative Jar Jar Binks was approaching the Senate Building in an airspeeder when he received

38

a transmission from the Senate Communi-
cations Center.

"This is the Coruscant Security Force. We
have you on our screen now. Please
identify."

"Mesa Jar Jar Binks, Associate Planetary
Representative for Naboo," replied Binks.

"Welcome, Representative Binks. Please
give us your height and position."

"Mesa six foot five and sitten up front,"
answered Binks.

What made Jar Jar finally speak out about all
the abuse he's endured?

He was inspired by the #MeesaToo
movement.

40

Did you know Luke milks thala-sirens without their consent?

How dairy!

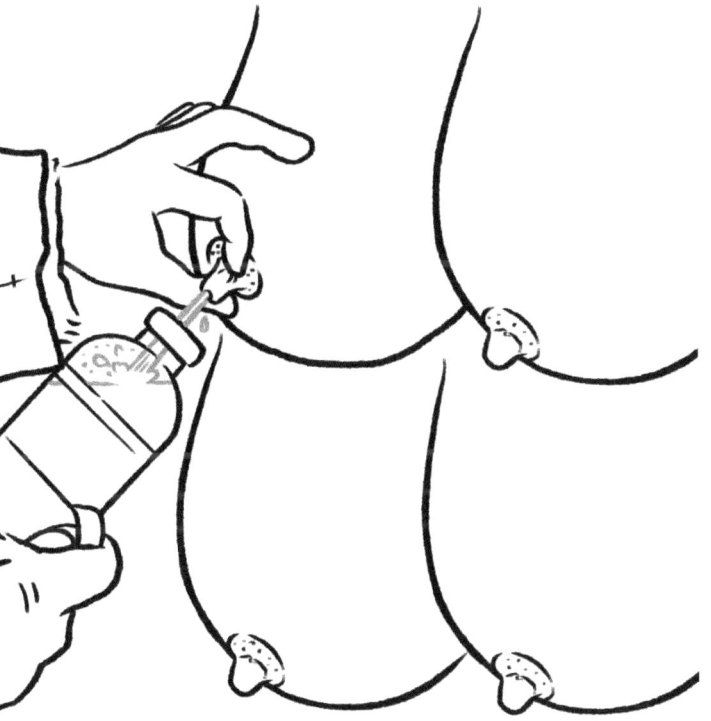

What's big and smelly and sprays shit across the Southern Dune Sea of Tattooine?

The other end of the Sarlacc.

"...and that's the Great Shit of Carkoon."

Jizz Wailers and Slave Dancers

Why does everyone tell Figrin D'an to smile more?

He has resting Bith face.

Why didn't Figrin D'an start playing the kloo horn until he was an adult?

When he was younger, he didn't have a kloo.

* * *

Why does the sperm bank pay Figrin D'an more than other donors?

His jizz is the best in the galaxy.

* * *

Joh Yowza, the jizz-wailing lead singer of the Max Rebo Band, approaches a Twi'lek dancer after a gig at Jabba's Palace.

"Hey, baby. You like jizz?"

The Twi'lek dancer throws her drink in Joh Yowza's face and storms off.

"What the hell was that all about?" he asks aloud.

"Didn't you hear?" says Max Rebo, the bandleader. "We're not supposed to call it 'jizz' anymore."

"We're not?" says Joh Yowza, surprised.

"Apparently it's offensive," says Max. "We're supposed to call it 'jatz' now."

"I had no idea," says Joh Yowza. "Thanks for the heads-up!"

Joh Yowza turns and notices an Askajian dancer standing alone in a corner of the room. He decides to try his luck again.

"Hey, baby. You like jatz?"

"Oh yes!" replies the Askajian. "I love jatz! Why do you ask?"

"Because," says Joh Yowza, "I'd love to jatz all over those tits!"

* * *

Never ask an Askajian's husband for help.

He's already dealing with more than he can handle.

* * *

How are Askajian women different than banthas?

I can think of half a dozen reasons.

* * *

What do you call an Askajian bounty hunter?

Boobie Fett.

* * *

Jabba the Hutt's Askajian dancer, Yarna d'al' Gargan, is running late. She rushes into

Jabba's Palace completely out of breath. Jabba is furious, until he notices Yarna's two black eyes.

"Yarna! What happened??? You look terrible! Who beat you up like that?!?!?"

"Beat me up?" says Yarna. "Nobody did! My stupid speeder broke down and I had to jog all the way to work!"

Why does Jabba keep an Askajian woman around him at all times?

To show that he can focus on six things at once.

Why doesn't Darth Maul get along with Askajian women?

They always go tit for tat.

*   *   *

An Askajian woman finds a lump under one of her breasts and seeks the attention of a medical droid.

"Don't worry," says the droid. "That's just your kneecap."

*   *   *

What happens when you motorboat an Askajian woman's lower breasts?

Cunnilingus.

*   *   *

Tail-Heads
and Sleemos

Why do female Twi'leks wear headdresses?

To cover their assholes.

* * *

Why did Twi'leks ban rectal thermometers on their home world of Ryloth?

Because they cause brain damage.

* * *

What goes "FLOPPITY-FLOPPITY-CRRAACK"?

A Twi'lek hitting his head on the sidewalk.

* * *

What's the best part about killing a Twi'lek prostitute?

The second hour is free!

* * *

What smells worse than a day-old lobster bib?

A fifty-year-old Bib Fortuna.

*   *   *

What's long, white, and smells like pork?

Bib Fortuna's finger.

What do you call it when a Twi'lek licks a Hutt's dirty butthole?

An Outer Rim job.

* * *

What's the best way to fuck a Hutt?

Roll it in flour and go for the wet spot.

* * *

Why does Watto have wings?

So he can rise above the crowd when he's bidding on slaves.

* * *

Why is Watto's nose so big?

Because air is free.

*   *   *

Watto, feeling very ill, is lying in what he
believes to be his deathbed. His slaves and
droids surround him, offering comfort in
what may be his final moments. Gasping for
breath, Watto speaks.

"Shmi, my loyal Shmi, are you there?"

"I am here, my master, as I always have
been," Shmi reassures him.

"And what about your son, Anakin? Are you
there, Ani?"

"I'm here, Watto," young Anakin responds.

"And my droids, are they here, too?"

"Yes they are," Shmi replies.

Suddenly, Watto bolts out of bed and
shouts, "THEN WHO'S WATCHING THE
SHOP?!!"

* * *

What happens when a Toydarian with an erection flies into a wall?

He breaks his nose.

* * *

How do you start a Toydarian parade?

Roll a wupiupi down the street.

* * *

How was Beggar's Canyon formed?

A Toydarian dropped a wupiupi down a womp rat hole.

* * *

Why do they smear shit on the walls at a Trandoshan wedding?

To keep the flies off the bride.

How do you get a Trandoshan pregnant?

Cum on her feet and let the flies do the rest.

*   *   *

Scum and Villainy

"You really shouldn't shit where you eat."

* * *

What do you call a Gamorrean Guard in a sleeping bag?

A pig in a blanket.

* * *

What did the stormtrooper say to the Gamorrean?

Come out with your hams up!

* * *

Did you hear about the Gamorean guard who jumped on a thermal detonator to save everyone in Jabba's Palace?

He was blown to bacon bits.

* * *

How do you tell the difference between an Ugnaught and a Gamorrean?

That's easy. Gamorreans smell like shit, and Ugnaughts smell like Gamorreans.

How do you save a drowning Geonosian?

Take your foot off its head.

How do Geonosians cure constipation?

They bug the shit out of you.

How does a clone trooper kill a Jedi Knight?

He shoots him in the temple.

*   *   *

Why can't stormtroopers aim?

The Empire's IT department blocked AOL.

*   *   *

68

"Execute Order 69."

*   *   *

Which stormtroopers wear the biggest helmets?

The ones with the biggest heads.

*   *   *

Whose grandson grew up to become the first Death Star commander?

Grandma Tarkin's.

*   *   *

What do Separatists eat for breakfast?

Count Dookula.

*   *   *

Scrap Piles
and Rust Buckets

Does a droid ever cuddle after sex?

No, he just screws, nuts, and bolts.

What is R2D2 short for?

He's got little legs.

Why is there a man inside of C-3PO?

Because C-3PO is gay.

Why does R2D2 have a little man inside of him?

Because R2D2 is a little gay.

Why do kids love R2D2 so much?

Because every kid dreams of owning a robot with a little person crammed inside.

*   *   *

How does a starship get into a relationship?

It finds its bae.

*   *   *

Why did Han Solo park the Millennium Falcon inside an asteroid?

He thought it was a parking meteor.

*   *   *

What do you call a starship that's soft, whiney, and addicted to social media?

The Millennial Falcon.

After being rescued from Jabba the Hutt, Han Solo approaches C-3PO and tells him he needs a favor.

"I'm going out for drinks with Lando and Chewie tonight. Head over to the cantina and save us a spot at the bar."

"I'm terribly sorry, Captain Solo," replies C-3PO, "but I'm afraid the cantina doesn't allow droids at the bar."

Han thinks for a moment, then hands C-3PO some money. "Go get yourself a disguise. Put on some clothes, maybe a wig. Be creative."

"But," says C-3PO, nervously, "what if my disguise doesn't work?"

"Are you kidding? That place is a freak show. You'll blend right in."

C-3PO heads to the marketplace and purchases a long, blonde wig, makeup, earrings, a sexy dress, fishnet stockings, and high heels. He puts on his disguise and enters the cantina. The bartender smiles.

"Hey, gorgeous! Have a seat in the VIP section and I'll be right with you!"

"Actually," says C-3PO, "I'd prefer to stay here at the bar."

"Sorry, sweetheart," says the bartender, "but I don't fuck sex droids at the bar."

* * *

Rebel Scum

Who leads the Rebellion, fights fabric pests, and smells like your grandma?

Mon Mothball.

*   *   *

How did the Rebel Alliance get Jek Porkins to join their cause?

Piece of cake.

*   *   *

What made the Death Star trench run at the end of *Episode IV* such a heavy scene?

Porkins.

*   *   *

Why did Porkins want to become a pilot?

There's zero gravity in space.

*   *   *

What kind of starfighter did Porkins fly?

An XL-Wing.

*   *   *

What was the last thing to go through Porkins' mind when his X-Wing exploded?

His teeth.

*   *   *

Why did Luke go to Cloud City?

To give his father a hand.

*   *   *

Why was Luke in a hurry to leave after his duel with Darth Vader on Bespin?

He was afraid the second-hand shop might be closing soon.

*   *   *

How did the Rebels greet Luke when he returned from Cloud City?

They gave him a hand.

Why couldn't Lando escape the Sarlaac by himself?

He needed a Han.

*   *   *

Why does Alderaanian food taste so bad?

Everything is overcooked.

*   *   *

Why did Princess Leia kiss her brother?

Because George Lucas is a pervert.

*   *   *

Why was Leia unsatisfied in bed?

Because Han always shot first.

* * *

Why does Princess Leia give Han Solo so many blowjobs?

She has a thing for rebel's cum.

* * *

Which moon was first explored by Ferrixian mechanic Bix Caleen?

The moon of Andor.

* * *

What happened when Lando fucked Lobot?

Gunter.

* * *

Finn, feeling absolutely famished after waking up from his Kylo-induced coma, wanders the Raddus in search of something to eat. His nose leads him to a massive room filled with Resistance leaders and members of the crew drinking and conversing around what appears to be a delicious seafood buffet. Finn tiptoes in and helps himself to some food before spotting Poe standing at the back of the room.

"Poe! Why didn't you tell me you guys were having a party?!"

"Shhhh! This isn't a party," whispers Poe. "This is a memorial service. Didn't you hear? Admiral Ackbar was killed in the explosion on the bridge. They plan to scatter his remains amongst the Mourning Shrines of Mon Cala. What the hell did you think this was?"

"I don't know," says Finn, "but the fried calamari is delicious!"

* * *

Hokey Religions

Did you hear about the anxious Padawan?

He became a great Jedi worrier.

Why are the Jedi against circumcision?

They believe in being one with the foreskin.

Why did everyone stare at Qui-Gon during his funeral?

He had a smoking hot body.

What's the best defense against an attack by Jango Fett?

Mace.

* * *

What did Anakin do to keep his Jedi vow of celibacy?

He got married.

* * *

With no one else to turn to, Anakin Skywalker seeks relationship advice from Supreme Chancellor Palpatine.

"Chancellor, whenever I'm making love to Padmé, I can't get her to cum at the same time as me. I don't know what to do."

"Here's what you do," says Palpatine. "Keep your lightsaber under your pillow. Just as you are about to blow your load, ignite your saber and wave it above your head, commanding all the powers of the force to levitate the bed and shake the very walls of Padmé's chamber! Surely, she will succumb to your power."

"Thank you, Chancellor. I shall try it tonight." With that, Anakin bids Palpatine farewell and hurries to Padmé's apartment.

Later that night, Chancellor Palpatine receives an urgent message from Padmé. Anakin is in the hospital, and he's asking for the Chancellor.

As Palpatine rushes into the room, he sees Anakin lying in bed, wincing in pain.

"Anakin, what happened to you?"

"Well, Chancellor, I put my lightsaber under my pillow, just like you said. Padmé said she wanted to sixty-nine, so we sixty-nined. Then, just as I was about to cum, I whipped out my lightsaber, levitated the bed, and shook the walls."

"And?" says Palpatine?

"And," says Anakin, "she bit the tip of my dick off and farted in my face!"

*　*　*

While leading an army of clone troopers into battle, a Jedi General senses a drop in his men's morale. In an attempt to rally the troops, the Jedi raises his lightsaber above his head and cries out to the soldiers.

"Men, did we come here to die?!"

"No sir!" responds one of the clone troopers. "We came here yester-die!"

*　*　*

What is Luke short for?

A stormtrooper.

*　*　*

Why did Luke find it hard to concentrate while training on Dagobah?

Because he could feel Yoda's little green dick poking him in the back the whole time.

Why did Yoda come off like a jerk to Luke when they first met?

If you were sitting in a filthy swamp with Frank Oz's hand up your ass, you'd be grumpy too!

*   *   *

Din Djarin takes Grogu to the Forge, where the Armorer has just constructed a Mandalorian codpiece for the foundling.

"Din Grogu, I present to you your next piece of armor, forged from scraps of beskar generously donated by fellow members of the Tribe. May this Mandalorian steel protect you as you grow both stronger and wiser."

Without hesitation, Grogu grabs the codpiece, stuffs it into his mouth, and swallows it whole.

"Grogu!" shouts Din Djarin, shocked and embarrassed by the foundling's unaccept-able behavior.

The Armorer, feeling highly disrespected, addresses Din Djarin. "Your foundling clearly has much to learn. If this sort of behavior continues, Grogu may find himself banished from the Tribe."

Din Djarin begs the Armorer for forgiveness. "I'm sorry. Please don't blame Grogu. We should have stopped for breakfast first…"

"Enough!" shouts the Armorer. "There is no excuse for such insolence."

"You're right," says Din Djarin. "I take full responsibility for the foundling's actions. I hope you'll consider giving him a second chance."

After taking some time to think, the Armorer agrees, reluctantly. "I shall give Din Grogu a second chance, but not today. Wait for the foundling to pass the beskar codpiece, then return to me. I will have something prepared for him, but only if he is ready."

"He'll be ready," promises Din Djarin.

"Very well, Din Djarin. But I must warn you, if Grogu fails a second time, his training shall come to an end, and he will be banished from the Tribe."

Din Djarin nods. "This is the way."

After three long days, Grogu finally passes

the beskar codpiece, so Din Djarin takes him to see the Armorer once more.

"I hope the foundling has learned his lesson."

"He won't make the same mistake again," replies Din Djarin. "Isn't that right, Grogu?"

Grogu nods in agreement.

"Then come, Din Grogu. Let us see if you are ready."

This time the Armorer presents Grogu with a newly forged pauldron, but before the Armorer even has a chance to speak, Grogu snatches the beskar armor from her hands and tries to shove it up his ass. He struggles for a moment, then gives up and tosses the pauldron onto the floor. The Armorer is appalled and demands an explanation.

"Well," says Din Djarin, "ever since Grogu swallowed that codpiece, he's been measuring things first."

*   *   *

Why does Rey suck at baseball?

She can't remember where home is.

*   *   *

What did it take for Leia to survive floating through space without a spacesuit?

Three hundred million dollars and a bad idea.

*   *   *

Sorcerer's Ways

* * *

What makes Senator Palpatine such an untrustworthy politician?

He's full of Sith.

* * *

How many Sith Lords does it take to screw in a lightbulb?

None. They prefer the dark.

* * *

Where does Emperor Palpatine keep his Imperial Armies?

Up his Imperial sleevies.

* * *

Why should you never make fun of Darth Maul's height?

He has a short temper.

*   *   *

Why is Darth Maul so short?

Because Obi-Wan sliced him in half.

*   *   *

What's that wretched smell coming from
the Naboo Plasma Refinery's reactor shaft?

Darth Maul's rotten ass, dick, balls, and feet.

How many younglings does it take to paint
the Jedi Temple?

Depends how hard you force throw them.

What's the difference between younglings and onions?

Anakin cries when he's slicing onions.

*   *   *

What do you call a dead youngling with no arms or legs lying at the entrance to the Jedi Temple?

Matt.

*   *   *

How did Padmé describe her trip to Mustafar?

She said it was breathtaking.

*   *   *

What's the difference between Anakin and a Whopper?

A Whopper doesn't scream while it's being flame broiled.

* * *

Why did Obi-Wan leave Anakin on Mustafar?

Because Anakin was a hot mess.

* * *

After the best surgical droids in the galaxy fail to save Anakin Skywalker's severed legs, Emperor Palpatine breaks the news to Anakin.

"Anakin, I have good news and bad news. The bad news is we were unable to reattach your legs."

"What's the good news?" asks Anakin.

The Emperor smiles. "You and I wear the same size boots!"

Why did no one laugh at the joke about Luke and Leia's birth?

The delivery was bad.

* * *

Why didn't Anakin attend Padmé's funeral?

He's not much of a mourning person.

* * *

What did Darth Vader say when James Earl Jones died?

Nothing.

John Szeluga is a comedian most recognized for his work as a comedy writer, producer, and performer on the hit TBS hidden camera series *Impractical Jokers*. He also produced and co-hosted the *Super Live Adventure Podcast,* and co-authored *The Best Fantasy Football Punishment Playbook*.

To learn more about John and sign up for his mailing list, visit JohnSzeluga.com.

Christopher J. Sorrentino (aka Pizza Plazm) is an illustrator best known for his ReelGhostbusters project. He's contributed art to *Impractical Jokers*, Shapeshift Records, the Official Chicago Bluesmobile, and the Staten Island Shakespearean Theatre. Chris also co-hosted the *Super Live Adventure Podcast*, and is an occasional comedic performer and actor.

Visit PizzaPlazm.com for bookings and commissions.